£4 -

The Apple Source Book

Particular Recipes for Diverse Apples

Common Ground

First published by Common Ground in 1991
Reprinted 1991, 1994

Common Ground
41 Shelton Street
London WC2H 9HJ

ISBN 1 870364 10 4

Cover design Stephen Turner
Designed and typeset in Times on an Apple Macintosh by
Stephen Turner and Jane Kendall at Common Ground
Printed by Wincanton Print, Somerset.
Sylvancoat chlorine free, recycled paper.

CONTENTS

ACKNOWLEDGEMENTS

Common Ground offers grateful thanks to all the contributors for being so generous with their thoughts, their recipes and their enthusiasm.

We are grateful to the Department of the Environment, Countryside Commission, Calouste Gulbenkian Foundation and others for their vital support of the Local Distinctiveness and Save Our Orchards campaigns.

Common Ground, charity no: 326335, London.

A CASE FOR VARIETY

In Britain we can grow the best apples in the world. Over the years we have bred or chanced upon hundreds of varieties which suit the vagaries of our climate, the mysteries of locality and our taste buds.

Our inheritance is an amazing one. Dabblers (people who plant pips) have given us our two most successful varieties - the Bramley and the Cox's Orange Pippin; farmers and nurserymen, such as the Laxtons, and professional plant breeders have crossed and created hundreds of others. Many have simply been found in woodland and hedgerow. Of the six thousand varieties that we have grown, about nine are readily available in most shops, and these same few varieties can be bought all over the world. In our local food shop in Covent Garden (once the fruit market of the world) we are only offered red or green apples.

From the wild crab apple we have created an amazing diversity but in half a life time we have squandered this cultural inheritance. Monoculture has taken over our countryside and monotony our shops.

Yet we should be as proud of the orchards - as protective of the hills and valleys and people which support them, and as imaginative about the foods, drinks, songs and stories which they generate - as the French are of their different vineyards and wines.

Common Ground has used the apple as a symbol of variety. The purpose of this book is to encourage the cultivation of local varieties in their season for local use. To grow and to be able to buy the Devonshire Quarrenden in Devon, the Blenheim Orange in Woodstock and the Galloway Pippin in the Borders reinforces local culture and enhances local distinctiveness.

The same arguments should be made for other fruits, vegetables, breads, cheeses and so on. They also apply to most other things which are becoming bland and universal, from our houses and high streets to our forests and fields.

The tragic loss of traditional orchards continues. Something like two thirds of our orchard area has disappeared in the last thirty years. Traditional orchards are distinctive in our landscapes. They are cultural landmarks, the source of genetic variety, local recipes and customs. They are beautiful places to look at and to be in and are havens for wild life.

What is Kent without its 60 foot high cherry trees, its magnificent cobnut plantations, pears, plums and apples, Gloucestershire without its perry pears, the Vale of Evesham without its plums, Shropshire without its hedgerow damsons, Devon and Somerset without their cider orchards?

Apple Day on October 21st, is an annual national celebration of the diversity of apples and other tree fruit which can be grown in this country. In 1990 Common Ground initiated Apple Day in the Old Apple Market in Covent Garden. But apples and orchards should be celebrated in their place. We invite you to celebrate Apple Day on or around October 21st, by simply making an apple feast in your home and/or by supporting the growing number of groups up and down the country who are mixing pleasure with the business of saving old orchards and creating new ones for school, city and community.

This book is offered in the hope that it will encourage inquisitiveness and experimentation. The same recipe will give different tastes and textures depending on the varieties of apples you use, in their season.

We share a land of extraordinary variety, rich in buildings, landscapes, people and wild life, with old and new cultural associations. That richness of local distinctiveness, the intimate relationship between place and culture, needs constant tending.

Remember, when you next buy a pound of apples, that the apple you eat is the landscape you create. We all have some responsibility and a little power to change things. What sort of countryside do you want? It is more than a matter of taste.

Angela King and Sue Clifford
Common Ground,
August 1991

"The fruite of Apples do differ in greatness, forme, colour and taste; some covered with a red skin, others yellowe or greene, varying indefinitely according to the soyle and climate; some very great, some little, and many of a middle sort; some are sweet or tastie, or something sower; most be of a middle taste betweene sweete and sower, to which to distinguish I thinke it impossible; not withstanding I heare of one that intendeth to write a peculiar volume of Apples, and the use of them..."

John Gerarde 1597.

AN APPLE FOR ALL SEASONS

With Bramleys on sale all year round, we have nearly lost all notion of the seasons and successions of different cooking apples that were a traditional part of country life, a hundred or even fifty years ago. Modern commercial storage has given us a sharp fresh cooker, even until July, which is something that our grandparents would have envied and never have been able to buy in markets, but it has also left us with little choice. Few people now know of, let alone try the dozens of varieties that used to grow all over Britain in gardens and orchards and provided a diversity of qualities from the codlins picked at the beginning of August to the very last of the 'late keepers' from the store after Easter.

It was in Victorian England that the notion of a culinary variety, one specifically grown for the kitchens and often especially valued for a particular dish became firmly entrenched in our culture. Definite opinions were then held as to which were the best varieties for making apple sauce, apple dumplings, jelly or pies and particularly which were the best plainly baked. Summer codlins were ideal and provided the first baked apples of the new season. Keswick Codlin and Early Victoria will quickly rise up like a frothy soufflé, and need no embellishments except perhaps a little sugar and a dribble of cream, but they were too juicy and insubstantial for pies and charlottes. One had to wait for the autumn ripening apples, such as Golden Noble, which is sharper, keeps a little of its form when cooked and so filled the pie with soft, golden fruit. It has a distinct flavour that can stand on its own, and the purists did not permit any distraction from cloves or lemon peel in a pie of Golden Noble.

For apple sauce Ecklinville Seedling, was prized for its smooth, savoury quality and the cider apple, Foxwelph with a 'rough, piquant flavour' also made a fine accompaniment to the Michaelmas goose, or roast leg of pork, In a more delicate style there was juicy Hawthornden and the Reverend W Wilks. These were followed by the large and angular Warner's King, suitable for most uses but not Apple Charlotte, which called for an apple that would make a stiff purée. Blenheim Orange was requested by the cooks. This is usually thought of as a dessert apple, but picked early it cooks well and will make a firm sauce for the moulded Charlotte.

Then came the late maturing apples, which were not picked until October and kept until the spring. The Victorian favourite was Dumelow's Seedling, which was sold in the markets as Wellington and is still to be found in old orchards. It has a translucent quality, good for pies and makes a delicious creamy, brisk baked apple or sauce, almost as sharp as a Bramley, but not quite so forceful. Dumelow's was overtaken at the beginning of this century by the larger and heavier cropping Bramley's Seedling, which at first was favoured for dumplings but soon became recommended for every kind of dish. Alas, Bramleys are now picked as early as August, but these 'thinnings' are immature, sour and starchy compared with the robust flavour of fruit left to develop properly on the tree. Not all late varieties are as strong. Many, like Annie Elizabeth, of the Midlands, are mild, it needs no sugar and was claimed to be the best of all for making a dish of stewed apples, because 'the quarters never break'.

Culinary varieties are distinguished from dessert apples by higher levels of acidity, as well as their larger size. The intensity and proportions of acid and sugar, in the main provide the flavour and the amount of acid determines the cooking properties. Generally the more acidic the apple is, the more easily it will cook and form a purée. Less sharp apples tend not to break down so readily and slices will retain their shape, but if the apple contains too little acid it will cook poorly. The structure of the flesh is another factor. Summer codlins, which 'size up' quickly and have loosely textured flesh with a good deal of water, will cook swiftly and often to a froth. Firm fleshed, late maturing varieties, such as Norfolk Beefing are less juicy and hold their form. Indeed, this was recommended for drying and was also used for making Norfolk Biffins, a popular Victorian sweetmeat, which was sold at the fruiterers to be taken home and eaten with sugar and cream. It was a speciality of Norwich bakers, who cooked the apples in the bread ovens after the bread had been removed. An iron plate was placed on top to gradually squeeze the air out, but since the apples are tough skinned they did not burst and thus sealed in, the flesh became rich and sweet. The same effect can be achieved by a very long baking at the lowest possible oven setting and the resulting 'Biffins' taste almost as if cinnamon flavoured.

The quality of the apple will be affected by the locality in which the fruit is grown and the year. Many Scottish and northern varieties of high culinary repute often lack acidity in southern gardens and are rather bland. Lord Derby, for instance, which arose in Cheshire, remains green and sharp until Christmas in the north, but in Kent is at its best in September and soon loses its acidity and appeal. On the other hand, James Grieve is a valued eating apple in southern gardens, but if deprived of sun is very sharp and in the north regarded as a cooking apple.

The way in which an apple cooks also depends to an extent upon when it is used and how it is stored. Windfalls and early picked fruit will be sharper and cook more easily than those harvested in their proper season. Even after picking, all apples continue to develop, and if you have your own trees or buy fruit from a Farm Shop for storing over the winter, then you will find that cooking properties change as the season progresses. Kept in a frost proof garden shed or some other dark, cool equivalent of the old fashioned fruit store, the apple's acidity will fall and the sugar level rise. The fruit will cook more firmly and taste sweeter, but many old culinary varieties soon become flat and insipid. It was then that the cook brought lemon juice and spices to their aid to supply the lost acidity and give flavour. Modern commercial storage overcomes the problem and will maintain fruit in a state close to the condition that it was in when picked. Before the inventions of the refrigerated and controlled atmosphere strorage, varieties that remained sharp through the winter without any trouble were highly valued. Dumelow's Seedling was the most prized, lasting until the forced rhubarb or even the first gooseberries appeared and Bramley's too will keep sound in amateur conditions until the weather begins to warm up.

That apples matured and sweetened over the winter in the barn or store, however, meant that many, like Annie Elizabeth were dual purpose. Another was Forge from Sussex, which is still grown in its home territory of East Grinstead. A brisk cooking apple in September, it is sweet and quite perfumed by Christmas, and even a Bramley becomes a sharp eating apple by March.

In its prime, a good English cooker, nevertheless possesses plenty of 'bite' and savoury character so that it can offset the richness of pork or game. Cooking itself ameliorates sharpness and if apple is to contrast with buttery pastry and zing through the sugar and cream, it needs to have plenty of flavour and piquancy to begin with. Bramley's Seedling's greatest virtue must surely be that no matter how much sugar, cinnamon, lemon peel or cloves a recipe demands, it will still emerge tasting strongly of apple. Delicate, mild flavoured cooking apples are easily swamped and best used in very simple ways. Similarly if one uses a dessert apple, such as a Cox, in a recipe it will be more interesting if cooked early and sharp.

Puddings such as an open tart, a Tarte aux Pommes, call for an apple that keeps its shape, yet is also richly flavoured, and here the familiar English cooker falls short of the requirements. French cooks use Reine des Reinettes, which is another name for our King of the Pippins. This is a variety that became widely distributed over Europe and thereby gathered up numerous synonyms. Grown in the warmer French climate it is larger and more colourful than in England, but is still to be found in Herefordshire as Prince's Pippin, and many old gardens have a tree of King of the Pippins. A September to October eating apple, it always has an underlying astringent quality and thus cooks well, Reinette du Canada is also favoured on the continent for Tarte aux Pommes which is similar to Blenheim Orange, but ripens later. Both are best used early in their seasons, since with keeping they develop their characteristic dessert qualities and then tend to be bland when cooked.

These, however, are not readily available, but many Farm Shops sell Newton Wonder and this is grown in hundreds of gardens. Not as acidic and aggressive as a Bramley, it is good used raw in vegetable salads, where the crisp, sharp, fruity taste is not overwhelmed by the vinaigrette dressing. A large Newton Wonder is just right for baked red cabbage, it can add plenty of flavour grated into stir-fried cabbage, and chopped apple greatly improves the bread and herb stuffing for the Christmas turkey.

Fresh fruit salads, on the other hand, ask for the best dessert apples, those with intensely aromatic rich flavours - a ripe Cox's Orange Pippin, Sunset, Holstein, Ribston Pippin and Orleans Reinette in the autumn - and well ripened they will have plenty of colour. Later in the season there is Ashmead's Kernel with its sweet sharp taste reminiscent of fruit drops and the robust Suntan and Tydeman's Late Orange. Plenty of interest can be provided in August and September by Discovery, Miller's Seedling, bright red Worcester Pearmain, which if really ripe is very sweet and tastes of strawberries, and Ellison's Orange with its lovely aniseed flavour.

Become familiar again with the diversity of flavours that English apples can offer. If you have the chance, experiment with different varieties and explore ways best suited to their particular qualities.

JOAN MORGAN the first woman to be a member of the Royal Horticultural Society Fruit and Vegetable Committee, is also a Founder Trustee of the Brogdale Horticultural Trust and author with Alison Richards of 'A Paradise out of a Common Field, the pleasures and plenty of the Victorian Garden', Century, 1990.

SOUPS AND SALADS

APPLE AND FENNEL SALAD

For this salad, try to find an aniseedy or fresh-tasting apple, such as Ellison's Orange, or a crimson-coloured one like Belle de Boskoop to point up the emerald of the fennel fronds. This salad is delicious either served on its own, or complementing cold pork, chicken or pâté.

2 Florence fennel bulbs
4 dessert apples
Dressing:
1 clove garlic
large pinch of sea salt
1 tsp fennel seeds
5 tsps virgin olive oil
1 tsp cider vinegar
1 tsp Meaux mustard
Serves 6

1. First make the dressing. Crush the garlic with the salt. Whizz the fennel seeds in the liquidizer to release their aroma, then add the garlic and the remaining ingredients and whizz together.

2. Cut the fennel bulbs in half lengthways, then cut across in thin slices. Depending on how much fennel frond there is, either mix into the salad or reserve for decoration. Leaving the pretty peel on the apples, cut, core and then slice them to match the fennel pieces.

3. Dress the salad, tossing well, to prevent the apples from browning.

PATRICIA HEGARTY from 'An English Flavour: Recipes from an English Country House and Garden', Equation, 1988. With her husband John, she owns and runs Hope End Hotel, Ledbury, Herefordshire where they grow and cook all their own vegetables and fruit.

A RUSSET SALAD FOR AN AUTUMN EVENING

The flesh of Egremont Russet apples (often called Russets for short) is smooth and creamy, with a nutty quality and their skins are the colour of autumn leaves - dull green, flecked with gold and blushed with orange. They are at their best from late September to the end of November.

The Egremont Russet flourishes in country gardens and is grown commercially on a small but diminishing scale. Russet apples do not cook well, neither do they take well to the cold store. They are best eaten soon after picking preferably accompanied by one of the milder, crumbly textured, Farmhouse cheeses such as Cheshire, Wensleydale or Caerphilly.

This is a salad with a real English flavour, to be served as a kind of high tea or light supper. Farmhouse cheese, sage and bacon combine with the apples to give a taste of old fashioned farmhouse fare, but with the light quality that has become more fashionable in recent years. The freshly picked 'wet' walnuts match the apples in their crisp texture and creamy flavour. Jacket potatoes or wholemeal bread are the best accompaniments.

2 large Russet apples
6 large celery sticks
8oz (225g) streaky bacon
6oz (175g) Farmhouse Cheshire cheese
4 tbsp olive oil
2 tbsp cider vinegar
1 tsp mustard powder
1 small onion, very thinly sliced
4 sage leaves, chopped
8oz (225g) freshly picked 'wet' walnuts, weighed before
shelling or 2oz (50g) shelled walnuts
1 bunch watercress
Serves 4.

Quarter, core and chop the apples, without peeling. Finely chop
the celery. Grill the bacon until it is crisp and crumble it. Cut
the cheese into small dice.

In a bowl, beat together the oil, vinegar and mustard powder.
Fold in the apples, celery, bacon, cheese, onion and sage.
Divide the salad between four plates. Shell and chop the walnuts
and scatter them over the top. Garnish with watercress.

GAIL DUFF from 'Food From the Country' by Gail and Mick
Duff, Macmillan, 1981. Gail Duff is a writer and broadcaster on
cookery, country life and local customs. [Note: Russet is a
general term for the browning of the skin - the Egremont Russet
is the best known, see also later recipe for Apple Sorbets which
includes Melcombe Russet.]

WALDORF SALAD

Waldorf salad is said to have been invented at the Waldorf Astoria Hotel in New York at the beginning of this century. It could be true as the Americans have a gift for 'meal' salads that is second to none. When made with chicken, this is a main course. But for vegetarians, or to go with a cold table, it is still very good without the chicken.

2 crisp apples of contrasting colours - Crimson Cox and Crispins for instance
1 head of celery
4oz (100g) walnut halves
8oz (225g) cooked chicken breast
juice of half a lemon
salt and pepper
¹/4pt (150ml) mayonnaise (home-made or a good quality commercial brand)
Serves 3-4

Core, but don't peel the apples and cut them into ½ inch (1cm) chunks. Wash the inner stalks of the celery and cut them into similar sized pieces. Chop the walnut pieces in half, saving some for decoration. Slice the chicken. Mix the apples, celery, walnuts and chicken with the lemon juice. Season the mixture and add mayonnaise. Stir well and chill for 30 minutes. Serve in lettuce cups decorated with walnut halves and celery leaves.

MICHAEL BARRY, co-presenter on BBC's 'Food and Drink' series and author of 'Exotic Fast Food for the Crafty Cook', Ebury Press, 1991.

APPLE AND CANNELINI BEAN SOUP

The apple gives the soup a gentle sweetness that is hard to define. This a reassuring and soothing soup, subtle and velvety without being bland. Use a well-flavoured eating apple [e.g. Millers Seedling, Cox's Orange Pippin, Tydeman's Late Orange, Ellison's Orange]

1½ onions, skinned and sliced
1½ oz (40g) butter
2 eating apples, peeled, cored and roughly chopped.
1½ x 14oz (400g) tins cannelini beans, drained and rinsed.
1 large sprig fresh tarragon
salt and freshly ground pepper
½ pt (275ml) milk
croutons to serve.
Serves 6

Fry the onion in the butter until soft without browning. Add the apples and continue to cook for 3 minutes, stirring occasionally. Add the cannelini beans, tarragon, ¾ pt (425ml) water, salt and pepper. Bring to the boil and simmer for 5 minutes. Cool slightly and liquidise. Return to the pan with the milk, and bring back to the boil. Taste and adjust seasonings. Serve scattered with crisp croutons.

SOPHIE GRIGSON from 'Food For Friends', Ebury Press, 1987. Sophie Grigson is an author, food writer and cookery columnist for the London Evening Standard and the Sunday Express Magazine.

CELERIAC AND APPLE SOUP

A delicate soup with pleasing subtle flavours, which is ideal for a summer lunch from Christopher Oakes at Oakes Restaurant, Stroud.

2-3oz (50-75g) butter
1 head of celeriac, peeled and chopped into cubes
5 Granny Smith apples, peeled and chopped into cubes
4 pints (2.25 litres) chicken or vegetable stock
salt
freshly ground black pepper
¼pint (150ml) double cream
celery leaves and diced apple, to garnish.
Serves 8

Melt butter in a heavy-based pan. Sweat the celeriac and apples without colouring for 5 minutes, or until soft. Add the stock and bring up to the boil. Reduce the heat and simmer slowly for 30-45 minutes. Purée the soup by processing it briefly in a food processor or blender.

Pass the purée through a sieve. Return the mixture to the pan and reheat; if it is too thick add more stock. Season to taste with salt and pepper. Swirl in the cream and garnish with the celery leaves and diced apple.

KEITH FLOYD from 'A Feast of Floyd', Grafton Books, 1990, writer, broadcaster and presenter of television cookery series.

SAVOURIES

ORCHARD TOASTED CHEESE

Lighter than many rarebits, this makes a lovely quick lunch dish and is pretty enough to serve at a party. Like all exceedingly simple dishes, its success depends almost entirely on using top quality ingredients.

I recommend clean, fresh tasting Lancashire cheese to balance a full-bodied Cheddar both farm-made using raw milk. I buy local Wiltshire produce: organic bread from Rushall Farm, Wiltshire cured ham from Sandridge Farm and mustard from Wiltshire Tracklements. My fruit supplies originate from neighbouring counties: Blenheim Orange or Queen Cox apples (both native to Oxfordshire) or Ashmeads Kernel (born and bred in Gloucestershire), and my favourite pear, Williams Bon Chrétien, raised in Berkshire. Muscat-scented white Italia grapes are the only import from overseas that I use for this dish. Patriotic cooks could substitute peppery bunches of watercress.

Only a splash of cider or apple juice is needed for the recipe - I suggest Julian Temperley's Burrow Hill cider, or apple juice from Aspalls or James White of East Anglia. Cider and apple juice are the right drinks to accompany the eating of Orchard Toasted Cheese; and I like to think that the ham might come from a pig which has roamed orchards and fed on windfall apples...

3-4 each ripe dessert apples and pears
a fine bunch of grapes (or 2 bunches watercress)
a few spoonfuls of cider or apple juice
the juice of half a lemon

4 large or 8 small not-to-thick slices of bread
a little mild mustard, preferably whole grain
4 large slices of ham, just carved from the bone
4-5 oz (100-150g) each Lancashire and Cheddar cheese,
grated and mixed
Serves 4 (or 8 as a snack)

Quarter the apples and pears, core them and cut into thick crescent moon slices. To prevent discolouration dip the slices in, or brush them with, the lemon juice mixed with 4 tablespoons of cider or apple juice. Shake off excess liquid, arrange on individual plates and garnish with clusters of grapes or clumps of watercress.

Toast the bread well on one side and lightly on the other. Splash the lightly toasted side with cider or apple juice, just a teaspoon or so per slice. Spread with mustard, cover with ham and top with the grated cheeses.

Cook under a medium-hot grill (avoid fierce heat: it spoils cheese making it stringy and tough). When the cheese is molten, hot and freckled golden-brown here and there, transfer the toasts to the prepared plates and serve. The idea is to nibble the fruit between mouthfuls of the hot toast, the clean tastes of the fruit providing an excellent foil for the richness of the ham and cheese.

PHILIPPA DAVENPORT adapted from 'Country Cook', Ebury Press, 1987. Food writer and journalist, she has a weekly column in The Financial Times and writes monthly for Country Living.

LEEK AND COCKPIT QUICHE

Our study has been of the local old orchards to try to reconstruct the part played by apples in the life and economy of the farms and workers. This was different from that played in the life of the country houses and larger rectories though apples were important there too. A farmer's wife with a team of men to cook for or a worker's wife with a large family had no time for sophisticated recipes. They seem to have had a sound, filling recipe for tarts, pies or roast apples or dumplings. Their success lay in judging and varying the filling according the the varieties in season or the kind of dish. Their judgement is seen in the composition of many of the old orchards in Yorkshire, where an acre of ground could contain as many as sixteen varieties of apple. These orchards seem to have been the domain of women to ensure a season from August to May, with apples ready for store or use all the time. Good storage was essential for many of these old varieties.

Among the first of the cooking apples would be the codlings, like the Keswick Codling, sharp flavoured, falling smoothly when cooked. They were used in the famous 'Codlings and Cream tarts' ordered by Parson Woodford for a 'good dinner' he gave at New College, Oxford at the end of July 1774. Variety increased during the early winter, with distinctively flavoured apples becoming mature. Goosberry with a taste reminiscent of gooseberries, Lemon Pippin with both flavour and smell having a citrous quality, Cockpit (Y) sharp tasting and keeping its shape well in a pie. Some of these varieties keep their scent when cooked, like Gravenstein and Green Balsam (Y), widely grown locally. One unusual variety quite specialised, was Wellington (or Dumelow's Seedling) ripening in November, it is juicy and sharp, and was popular for mincemeat. These are all moderate sized apples. Kept properly they will mature and store till Easter when the real keepers, like Northern Greening, come to their best. These are hard and sour earlier and are often wasted by the later owners of orchards who do not know how to treat them.

Yorkshire Greenings' alternative name, Yorkshire Goose Sauce (Y), suggests another use, but for apple sauce late in the season, many people now use Keswick Codlings, cooked and kept in the freezer.

The large apples, are best roasted or used in dumplings. Warner's King provides a change of taste from Bramleys, and in this area, Lane's Prince Albert keeps very well, retaining texture and flavour till quite late. Striped Beefing is another good keeper, though here rather outside its home area. But there is a difficulty, Yorkshire Beauty (which goes by different names in different places, such as Hawthornden) produces a fruit a pound or more in weight. Who today would welcome a dumpling with a good crust covering a pound of apple?

Some of the old apples are more interesting for their names than their flavour, Dog's Snout and Cat's Head. Others are frankly undistinguished, like Burr Knot, once widely grown round here. Backhouse's Flowery Town (Y) was once popular in the area but we find it very ordinary, though its pink flesh is quite attractive.

These notes are based on experience in using a few of the old apple varieties grown in Ryedale, North Yorkshire. We have learned the flavours of many apples, especially when properly stored to allow them to gain a true maturity. But selection is necessary. Some varieties fail to reach their best outside a limited area. Some have only an antiquarian interest. Carefully selected and grafted onto a stock appropriate to modern gardens, many could give a lively interest to apple dishes.

Why serve apple pies when you could serve 'Cockpit pie with a dash of Brownlees Russet'?

6oz (175g) shortcrust pastry
2-3 leeks
1-2 Yorkshire Cockpit apples (or what you will in season)
2 eggs
small ¹/₂ pt (275ml) milk
few sage leaves, finely chopped
a little grated Wensleydale cheese to taste
pepper and salt.

Line a suitable dish with pastry, chop leeks and parboil in slightly salted water, cool. Peel and chop the apples. Place the leeks and apples in quiche case. Beat the eggs, add milk, chopped sage, salt & pepper, pour over apples and leeks and sprinkle with grated cheese. Bake in the centre of a moderate oven 325F/160C/Gas 3, for 30-40 minutes. Try different varieties in season and rename the dish accordingly.

GEORGE AND BARBARA MORRIS are experts on apples surviving in Yorkshire.
[(Y) represents native Yorkshire varieties]

HEAVEN AND EARTH

The German kitchen has some particularly good potato recipes, including delicious pancakes made with raw grated potatoes and served with apples or stewed fruit; and an excellent dish known as "Himmel unde Erde" which mixes boiled potatoes with apples and crisp fried bacon. This mixture of fruit and vegetables, sweet and sour, is characteristic of northern country cooking - Holland, Belgium, Alsace, Czechoslovakia, Poland, and Scandinavia all have similar mixtures.

Immigrants to America, particularly the German and Dutch settlers in Pennsylvania, took their sweet-salt dishes with them and adapted the recipes to local ingredients. The resident Indians already used sweet maple syrup to dress their meat. Thence developed those peculiarly American dishes such as pumpkin and marshmallow pie to eat with the Thanksgiving turkey. Waffles with maple syrup and bacon, even the peanut-butter-and-jelly sandwich, belong to the same tradition.

The Europeans seem to use firm but sweet apples like reinettes for cooking. This makes an excellent supper or light luncheon dish.

2lb (1kg) potatoes
2lb (1kg) apples [such as King of the Pippins]
salt
8oz (225g) slab bacon in ¹/₄" (6mm) thick slices.
Serves 4 as a main course.

You need a large saucepan and a small frying pan.

If the potatoes are new and small, you merely need to wash them. If they are old, peel them closely and quarter them. Put them to boil in plenty of salted water. Peel and cut the apples into chunks the size of the potato pieces. Add them to the potatoes after 10 minutes. Finish cooking both together. By the time the potatoes are cooked the apples will be soft but still holding their shape. Meanwhile dice the bacon and fry it in its own fat. Drain the cooked apples and potatoes. Pile them into a hot dish and scatter the crisp bacon, with its cooking juices, over the top. Serve immediately.

ELISABETH LUARD adapted from 'European Peasant Cookery', Corgi, 1988. Elisabeth Luard is a cookery writer, contributing cookery editor of Country Living and writes a column in The Scotsman. She is also author of 'European Festival Food' and ' The Barricaded Larder'.

LEEK AND RUSSET MEDLEY WITH ALMONDS

Egremont Russets hold their shape well and have a nutty aromatic flavour, ideal for this blend of tastes and textures. Caraway was a popular flavouring for apple preserves in the seventeenth century.

1lb (500g) firm leeks
1lb (500g) Egremont Russets
3oz (75g) butter

salt & pepper
pinch caraway seeds
1/4 pt (150ml) chicken or vegetable stock
2oz (50g) split blanched almonds

Clean the leeks thoroughly, peeling away the outer skins, then slice them diagonally into chunks about ½" (1cm) wide. Peel, core and slice the apples. Melt 2oz (50g) butter in a heavy saucepan and sweat the leeks and apples in this for a minute or two, turning them till they are well coated in butter. Season, and dust with caraway seeds. Add the stock, cover and cook very gently for 10 minutes.

Meanwhile, melt the remaining butter and cook the almonds in it for a few minutes, until slightly browned. Spoon the leek and apple mixture into a serving dish and scatter with the almonds. This goes well with roast and grilled meat, especially pork, ham and bacon.

RUTH WARD is an apple enthusiast and food writer. Author of 'A Harvest of Apples', Penguin, 1988, on cookery, history and folklore of apples.

PORK CHOPS WITH APPLES

4 x ½" thick spare rib or loin pork chops
1 medium onion - chopped
5-6 Ribston Pippin apples - peeled and sliced
2 sticks celery - chopped

1 tbsp plain flour
8 fl oz (225ml) apple juice or dry cider
1 tsp thyme
1 tsp salt
1/4 tsp pepper
5 tbsp sour cream or Greek yoghurt
Serves 4

Heat a large ovenproof casserole over a high heat to sear the pork chops quickly. Remove them onto a plate.
Into the casserole add onions and celery - sauté until soft, stir in the flour.
Remove from heat adding apple juice or cider, thyme, salt, pepper and apples.
Add the pork chops to the mixture in the casserole.
Cover and cook in the oven at 325F/170C/Gas 3 until the pork is tender - about 1½ - 2 hours.
Remove from the oven and stir in sour cream or yoghurt before serving.

Adapted from 'Just What the Doctor Ordered' by Harriet Goodman and Barbara Morse, Arlington Books, 1983.

ANN AND ANDREW TANN run Crape's Fruit Farm, Aldham, Colchester, Essex growing over 150 varieties of apples. Discovery, Worcester Pearmain, St Edmund's Russet, Laxton's Fortune, Sunset and Ribston Pippin are some of the varieties available by mail order. Orders for Christmas should be made by October 1st, or earlier, each year.

GRILLED SAUSAGES WITH SAGE FRIED APPLE RINGS

While the Bramley's Seedling may be the most renown British cooking apple I have been trying some Spartan dessert apples in the kitchen. I was looking for an apple that did not fall apart when cooked and have tried baking and frying these sweet, red skinned apples with great success. Fried apple rings make a delicious accompaniment to grilled sausages especially when the sausages have been liberally spiced with sage.

1lb (450g) good pork sausages
3 medium Spartan dessert apples
fresh sage
1 tablespoon pork dripping or oil
Serves 4

Put the sausages on to grill. Wash and core the apples but do not peel them. Slice into rounds about ½" (1cm) thick. Fry the apple rings in the heated fat in a non stick frying pan until they are golden on both sides, this takes about 5-8 minutes and should be done over a medium heat. As the apple cooks their sugar caramelises so be careful they don't burn. Remove to a heated serving dish with the grilled sausages. Put the chopped sage leaves into the pan and stir them in the remains of the fat to release their flavour, sprinkle the sage over the sausages and serve the dish with a mound of buttery mashed potato.

THANE PRINCE is Cookery Editor for The Daily Telegraph where this recipe appeared on October 20th 1990.

DEVONSHIRE RABBITS

This is the recipe we use for our rabbits. The Tom Putt is just large enough, but Bramleys or Biffins would do. As an apple to eat Tom Putt isn't much good although, inevitably, some locals swear by it. I sell the trees of this variety and there is always a regular trade.

One of the oldest of all recipes is one that I have adapted and use here. The original will be found in 'De re coquinaria' by Coelius Apicius, under Pork and Matian apples. The Matian apple is mentioned first by Varro just before BC became AD. Columella tells us that it was called after C. Matius, the gastronome. It may be possibly be still around in the form of one of the Court Pendu type apples.

8 large Tom Putts
2 rabbits
1 onion, chopped
1 finger of grated ginger
10 cloves
2 pts (1 litre) dry cider and small glass cider
2oz (50g) butter
4oz (100g) walnuts
3 slices bread, chopped
pinch of salt to taste

1. Marinade both rabbits in 2 pints of cider with ginger and cloves, leave in cool pantry, turning 3 times over 3 days.
2. Take out and dry rabbits.

3. Joint rabbit number one.
4. Heat oven to medium hot.
5. Add salt to marinade.
6. Cook joints of rabbit number one in marinade for 40 minutes.
7. Meanwhile, brown rabbit number two in butter.
8. Take joints out of marinade and replace with rabbit number two, cook for 40 minutes.
9. Carve meat off joints and chop coarsely.
10. Take 8 Tom Putts or other large cookers and chop off caps and stalk ends.
11. Core apples and gently cut out extra flesh to make a cavity.
12. With sharp knife make a shallow cut round equators of apples.
13. Fry chopped onion in butter left from browning rabbit until transparent.
14. Add apple flesh, bread and cider from glass. Mash until stuffing consistency.
15. Add meat pieces and walnuts to stuffing mix and stuff apples. Replace caps. Put in oven for 10 minutes.
16. Remove whole rabbit from oven and put on hot serving dish.
17. Thicken cooking juices and pour some over whole rabbit. Put rest in gravy boat.
18. To help serving snip almost through segments of whole rabbit but leaving it in shape.
19. Serve whole rabbit surrounded by stuffed apples.

EVERARD O'DONNELL runs the Devonshire Apple Sanctuary, Red Hill Farm, Burlescombe, Tiverton, Devon where he grows 350 varieties of apples including many cider varieties and will graft to order.

CHICKEN BREASTS STUFFED WITH APPLE AND SAGE

8 chicken breast fillets with skins on
1 1/2oz (40g) butter
3 red skinned dessert apples [Worcester Pearmain, Devon-
shire Quarrenden]
1 tbsp quince jelly

For the stuffing:
1 small onion
1/2oz (10g) butter
2oz (50g) fresh white breadcrumbs
8oz (225g) curd cheese
fresh sage leaves or 1/2teasp rubbed dried sage
salt and freshly milled pepper
2 red skinned dessert apples
Serves 8

Partially loosen the skin on each chicken breast with fingertips
to form a pocket. Set aside while preparing the stuffing.
 Peel and finely chop the onion. Melt the butter in a saucepan,
add the onion and cook gently to soften. Draw off the heat and
stir in the breadcrumbs with a fork. Turn the curd cheese into a
mixing bowl. Add the breadcrumb mixture, the finely chopped
sage leaves (or rubbed sage) and a good seasoning of salt and
freshly milled pepper. Quarter, and core the apples leaving on
the skins, then grate coarsely and add. Mix thoroughly.

Take a dessertspoon of the stuffing and spoon into the pockets
under the chicken skin. Fold thinner ends of the breasts

underneath to form neat rounded shapes. Arrange close together in a well buttered fireproof dish. (Can be prepared ahead. Cover and refrigerate up to 8 hours.)

Heat oven to 180C/350F/Gas 4. Brush the chicken breasts with ½ oz (10g) butter, melted. Set in the heated oven and bake for 30-35 minutes or until golden brown. Meanwhile, peel, core and slice the apples. Melt the rest of the butter in a frying pan. Add the apple slices and pan fry for 2-3 minutes turning them over once or twice. Draw off the heat, add the quince jelly and stir until jelly is melted and apple slices are glazed.

Transfer chicken breasts to a heated serving platter. Add juices from the baking dish to the apple slices. Stir to blend. Then arrange apple slices and pan juices around chicken to serve.

KATIE STEWART is food editor of Woman's Journal and author of 'Entertaining with Katie Stewart', Pavilion Books, 1990.

PUDDINGS

A DEVONSHIRE CHARLOTTE OF APPLE AND PLUMS

I devised this charlotte in praise of Susan Bosence, the Devonshire craftswoman-artist whose resist-dyed, hand-printed cottons and silks unite colour, pattern, and fabric in rare mutual affinity.

Susan and 'Bo' Bosence inhabit eight undulating acres at the edge of Dartmoor, growing domestic bounty of organic fruits, vegetables, flowers, and herbs, tending a long-established orchard of "dessert and cooking apples mixed in with various ciders. It's likely", says Susan, "that we have the traditional Devon varieties - Allspice, Quarrenden, Oaken Pin, Crimson Costard, Star of Devon, Michaelmas Stubbard - but hardly any of the trees has been properly identified!"

Among the apples is a lone plum stock whose fruit, says Susan, "looks like a cross between Damson and Dittisham: its taste is on the sharp side, but ripening into 'fruitiness' with a hint of Victoria". Theirs is too high and exposed to be "true plum country", but several decades back, Susan and Bo would drive, each August , " down the long lane beside the Dart estuary to Dittisham," where the river bank shelters a "warm, almost maritime 'dip'", formerly filled with orchards of the rich, dark-crimson Dittisham Ploughman plum that has now become a rarity.

If Susan were making an apple charlotte, she would probably choose an early Blenheim ("I *think* I have one!"), as recommended by Joan Morgan. When pressed, by me, to select a

Devon variety from among her trees, she picked, for baking this mixture of apples with plum, the "sharp, Bramley-like" Michaelmas Stubbard with, to provide the sweet density which I like to find in a charlotte, a couple of pounds of Charles Ross, the Berkshire-bred, "slightly peachy" dessert and cooking variety of which Susan has one tree at the bottom of her kitchen garden. This is a charlotte for Michaelmas (late September/early October), when Susan's 'Damson-Dittisham' plums are ripe.

2lb (1kg) Charles Ross apples
1¹/₂lb (750g) Michaelmas Stubbard cooking apples
1¹/₂lb (750g) late-ripening red or dark crimson-skinned plums:
'Damson-Dittishams', or Laxton's Delicious, or one of the
'pure' Damsons
5oz (150g) butter
about 4oz (125g) golden granulated sugar
juice of 1 large lemon
¹/₂ loaf brown sandwich bread, 2 days old
icing sugar
crab-apple jelly, home-made if possible
double cream
Serves 4

Peel, core, slice apples; quarter and stone plums (leaving skins on). Place fruit, with a little water, 1oz (25g) butter, the sugar, and lemon juice in a large, heavy saucepan. Cook contents, first with and then without a lid, into a very stiff purée, stirring often to prevent burning. Cool; the result should be rather tart.

Clarify remaining butter and lightly brush a 2-pint (1.2-litre) charlotte mould with some of the resultant yellow oil; cut a circle of greaseproof paper to fit base of mould and press this into place. Thinly-slice three-quarters of the half-loaf, remove crusts, cut each slice in half lengthwise and lightly toast on both sides. Brush slices with clarified butter and run toast upright, slices slightly overlapping, round inside of mould. Fill bread case as full as possible with purée, cut and toast some wider, crustless slices to make a lid, brush with remaining clarified butter.

Place charlotte mould on a heavy baking sheet and bake at 400F/200C/Gas 6 for 20-25 minutes, until toast is well-browned. Let charlotte cool for 20 minutes, turn out onto a plate, peel away greaseproof. Dust sides lightly with icing sugar sifted through a tea-strainer, and present with crab-apple jelly and cream.

ALICE WOOLEDGE SALMON, who writes in Britain and America, is a founder-member of the British Guild of Food Writers. This recipe was first published, in a slightly different form, by House & Garden, March 1991.

APPLE AND GUAVA STRUDEL

I use a sharp cooker from my parent's orchard (variety unknown), but a good, early, sharp cooking apple would be ideal to contrast with the highly perfumed guava. Frozen strawberries can be used in this recipe, too, instead of guava.

2 large cooking apples, peeled (optional), but cored [Golden Noble]
2 small guavas, peeled and with central pulp removed (save for flavouring custards or cheesecake fillings)
juice of half a lemon

4oz (100g) large seeded raisins (not seedless)
stick of cinnamon
few allspice berries
2 cloves
$^1/_2$-1oz (14-25g) unsalted butter, melted
2oz (50g) wholemeal breadcrumbs, toasted
4 sheets filo pastry (strudel leaves)
2oz (50g) icing sugar (optional)
few drops bitter orange oil or rosewater (optional)

Place the guava, lemon juice, raisins, cinnamon, allspice berries
and cloves in a saucepan or microwave dish with a minimum of
cold water to avoid burning or sticking, and cook gently to soften
the fruit. Stir in breadcrumbs to absorb liquid. Add the raw
chopped apple (Golden Noble falls very quickly hence it is not
precooked, although other varieties may need to be cooked with
the guava). Place a sheet of pastry on an oiled baking tray and
brush lightly with butter, put another sheet on top and brush with
butter, repeat. Place the apple mixture in a long 'sausage' along
the length of the pastry. Brush the edges with more butter. Tuck
in the ends and roll up. Brush the top with remaining butter.
Bake at 400F/200C/Gas 6 for 15 minutes until golden brown.
Serve hot or cold with thick natural yoghurt.
You can ice the top if you like. Sift the icing sugar into a bowl
and mix with ½ tablespoonful of boiling water and a couple of
drops of orange oil/rosewater. Spoon over strudel.

JANETTE MARSHALL from 'All for One', Penguin, 1990.
She is an author and food writer with a particular interest in
health and food quality, currently working on the 'definitive'
diet and healthy eating book to be published 1992.

POMMES AU BEURRE

For these recipes I always use Cox's Orange Pippins.

I have never very greatly appreciated cooked apple dishes, but from the French I learned two valuable lessons about them. First, choose hard sweet apples whenever possible instead of the sour cooking variety which are used for English apple dishes. And secondly, if the apples are to be eaten hot, cook them in butter instead of in water. The scent of apples cooking in butter is alone more than worth the small extra expense.

For 2lb (1kg), then, of peeled and cored sweet apples, evenly and rather thinly sliced, melt 2oz (50g) of butter in a frying pan. Put in your apples, add 3 or 4 tablespoons of soft white sugar (vanilla flavoured if you like), and cook gently until the apples are pale golden and transparent. Turn the slices over very gently, so as not to break them, and if very closely packed, shake the pan rather than stir the apples. Serve hot; and I doubt if many people will find cream necessary. The delicate butter taste is enough.

LA TARTE AUX POMMES NORMANDE

Cook 1½ lb (750g) of sweet apples as for 'pommes au beurre'. Make a pâte sablée or crumbly pastry by rubbing 3oz (75g) of butter into 6oz (175g) of plain flour, a quarter-teaspoon of salt, and 3 teaspoons of white sugar. Moisten with 2 to 4 tablespoons of ice cold water. If it is still too dry, add a little more, but the less water you use the more crumbly and light your pastry will be.

Simply shape the pastry into a ball and immediately, without leaving it to rest or even rolling it out, spread it with your hands into a lightly buttered 8-inch flan tin. Brush the edges with thin cream or milk; arrange the apples, without the juice, in over-lapping circles, keeping a nicely shaped piece for the centre. Bake with the tin on a baking sheet, in a pre-heated hot oven at 400F/200C/Gas 6 for 30 to 35 minutes, turning the tin round once during the cooking. Take it from the oven pour in the buttery juices, which have been reheated, give another sprinkling of sugar, and return to the oven for barely a minute.

Although it is at its best hot, this pastry will not go sodden even when it is cold.

ELIZABETH DAVID from 'French Provincial Cooking', Michael Joseph, 1960 and Penguin, 1964. Elizabeth David is a self taught cook and food writer. Her books include: 'Mediter-ranean Food', 'French Country Cooking', 'Italian Food'and 'Summer Cooking'. [See also her essay 'Big Bad Bramleys' in 'An Omelette and a Glass of Wine, Penguin, 1986]

APPLE JOSEPH

Being a Lancastrian by birth I have a weakness for pies. Meat pies, potato pies, custard pies, fruit pies, I love them all but that is not to say I will eat any old pie. During the years I like to think that I've come to be something of a pie connoisseur and I know a good one from a poor attempt. I grade them from 1 to 10 and most bought pies rate between 4 and 7. The ultimate are those pies thin of crust, bulging with filling which I used to buy as a young man from a corner shop in Bolton.

I found a similar shop in Ashton-under-Lyne some years ago. It was close to a canal where we were filming for a Channel 4 series on wild flowers and each morning as soon as we arrived we would send the research assistant to place our orders to be collected at noon. Sitting on the canal side with flowering rush and arrowhead providing a feast for the eyes and a meat and potato pies followed by a juicy blackberry and apple pie providing for our inner needs is a memory I shall always cherish.

So, apples in a pie are obviously a favourite of mine and much as I have enjoyed pies baked by countless friends and gardening acquaintances I recommend a recipe tasted only recently baked by a German chef in an Irish hotel (The Dunloe Castle, nr Killarney, Co. Kerry). If it sounds a bit rum I hasten to add that Joseph Fassbender (the chef) insists on using an English Bramley for his pie, no other has quite the same acidity he assures me and that without a Bramley it is not his pie. Appropriately he calls it Apple Joseph!

1lb (500g) Bramley apples
2oz (50g) almonds
2oz (50g) sugar
2 cloves
breadcrumbs

Sweet Pastry:
8oz (225g) butter
4oz (100g) caster sugar

1 egg - beaten
13oz (375g) plain flour
pinch of salt

Mix together butter and sugar until very pale. Add beaten egg followed by plain flour and salt to make sweet pastry.

Peel 1lb (500g) of apples and cut very fine. Crush 2 oz (50g) almonds and add to apples with 2 oz (50g) sugar and 2 cloves. Mix in bowl until apples are moist.

Roll out pastry, put some breadcrumbs on it, add apple mixture and bake for 40 minutes at 400F/200C/Gas 6.

ROY LANCASTER is co-presenter of Channel 4's Garden Club, plantsman and plant hunter, Victoria Medalist of the Royal Horticultural Society, author and writer for Country Life, Woman and Home, etc.

BAKED APPLE & QUINCE DUMPLINGS

It is said that the apple which, in falling from its tree inspired Sir Isaac Newton, was a variety called Flower of Kent. It is also said that Newton's favourite dish was baked quinces. When I was writing for the National Trust on fruit and vegetable cookery, I cobbled together a recipe to combine both fruit. Flower of Kent apples are not native to Lincolnshire, where Newton lived at Woolsthorpe Manor, near Colsterworth, but Peasgood's Nonsuch is, and is perfectly suited to this recipe. Or you can cheat a little and use Bramleys, since they come from Southwell, just over the border into Nottinghamshire.

2 ripe quinces
honey to taste
1oz (25g) butter
12oz (350g) sweet shortcrust pastry
4 small cooking apples
1 egg, beaten

Peel and core the quinces, cut them up and stew with a little water over a low heat until soft. Purée them, together with enough honey to sweeten to your taste, taking into account that this mixture has to sweeten the apples too, and beat in the butter. Roll out the pastry and divide it into four squares. Peel and core the apples and put each in the centre of a square of pastry. Fill the cavities generously with the quince purée, then fold the pastry up and around to enclose the apples, pinching the edges together firmly with the help of a little water, or some of the beaten egg. Brush with more egg and arrange on a baking sheet before baking in a hot oven for 25-30 minutes. Serve hot, warm or cold, with thick cream and extra sugar if necessary.

NB If quinces are unobtainable use the fruit of the japonica or Japanese Quince (chaenomeles) instead, but you will need four times the quantity as they are so much smaller.

SIMONE SEKERS from 'The National Trust Book of Fruit and Vegetable Cookery', National Trust, 1991. She writes a cookery column in the Weekend Telegraph and Sunday Telegraph.

TARTE TATIN

Tarte aux demoiselles Tatin is both the trickiest and the most delicious of all apple pies. This recipe is the best version there is - tested and perfected by 15 teachers and 100 students at Leith's School of Food and Wine. It is best made with Bramley apples.

For the pastry:
6oz (170g) plain flour
2oz (55g) ground rice
5oz (140g) butter
2oz (55g) caster sugar
1 egg, beaten

For the topping:
2lb (1kg) cooking apples
4oz (110g) butter
4oz (110g) granulated sugar
Grated rind of one lemon

1. Set the oven to 375F/190C/Gas 5.
2. To make the pastry: Sift the flour and ground rice into a large bowl. Rub in the butter until the mixture looks like breadcrumbs. Stir in the sugar. Add the egg and bind the dough together. Chill while you prepare the top.
3. To make the topping: Melt the butter in a 10" (25cm) frying pan with a metal handle. Add the granulated sugar and take off the heat. Peel, core and thickly slice the apples. Arrange the apple slices over the melted butter and sugar in the base of the frying pan. Sprinkle on the grated lemon rind.

4. Place the frying-pan over a high flame until the butter and sugar start to caramelise (it will bubble up around the sides of the pan). Remove from the heat.

5. Roll the pastry into a thick (approx ¼"(5mm)) circle to fit the top of the pan. Lay it on top of the apples and press down lightly. Bake in the oven for 25-30 minutes.

6. Allow to cool slightly, turn out onto a plate and serve warm.

Note: If you do not have a frying pan with a metal handle cook the apples in an ordinary frying pan - let the butter and sugar mixture become well caramelized and tip in to an ovenproof dish. Cover with the pastry and then bake in the oven on a hot baking sheet.

PRUE LEITH is a writer, teacher and restaurateur, winner of the Veuve Clicquot Business Woman of the Year Award 1990. Leith's School of Food and Wine, 21 St Alban's Grove, London, W8 5BP.

CHEESE AND APPLE TARTLETS

Despite its northerly latitude, Scotland has had a long tradition of apple-growing, and until quite recently large areas of Clydesdale south-east of Glasgow, the Carse of Gowrie between Perth and Dundee, and Tweedside in the Borders were devoted to orchards. About twenty historic Scottish varieties are still in existence. Most of these can be traced back to particular counties or districts within Scotland.

This recipe is based on one from a Good Housekeeping book of 1955. It provides a good basis for experimenting with both apple varieties and cheeses as the ingredients are few and uncluttered with other flavourings.

Line patty tins with shortcrust pastry and prick. Half fill them with chopped apple, and sprinkle with sugar. Bake in a hot oven 425F/220C/Gas 7 until the apple is tender and the pastry beginning to brown - about 10 minutes. Remove from the oven and sprinkle with a layer of grated cheese and bake until the pastry is cooked and the cheese is golden brown - approximately 5 minutes. Serve hot or cold.

We would, of course, suggest Scottish apple varieties: James Grieve (an eater, but will cook well, probably most widely available), Hawthornden, White Melrose, Tower of Glamis, Galloway Pippin, Stirling Castle, Bloody Ploughman and Coul Blush depending on availability.

CRAIG AND CHRISTINE PILLANS have built up a collection of over 75 varieties of apples, including all the surviving pre-twentieth century Scottish varieties. Craig's booklet 'Historic Apples of Scotland' is available for £1.50 from Avondale, Church Lane, Utterby, Louth, Lincs, LN11 0TH.

APPLE MERINGUE

One short-crust pastry flan case baked 'blind' (This can be prepared in advance and frozen). Cooked and lightly sweetened

Bramley apple - spread ½" thick into pastry flan case.

Whip the whites of two eggs until stiff and add 4oz (100g) caster sugar to make the meringue. Spread this over the apple and cook on top shelf of oven at 300F/150C/Gas 2 until firm and lightly coloured. Serve with cream.

As for dessert apples, Geoffrey definitely prefers Cox's Orange Pippin with Wensleydale cheese and notes that the Egremont Russet makes an excellent landscape tree as well as being a good eater when well grown.

MARJORIE SMITH makes this for herself and her husband Geoffrey Smith, plantsman, author and broadcaster.

AUTUMN PUDDING WITH WILDING APPLES

Wild apples don't really deserve their reputation for forbidding sourness. True crab-trees (distinguishable by their spiny branches) do indeed have small, acrid, bullet-hard fruits that are only really useful as providers of pectin in jam-making. But most feral apples are what are commonly known as 'wildings', sprung from the seed of discarded domesticated apples. They carry all the genetic variety of the family, and are often mild and bulky enough to be edible raw. Amongst them you can find apples with flavours touched with gooseberry, lemon and pear, with colours from straw yellow to plum red, and with a range of textures to match. The most seductive are those occasional fruits which are scented with quince, and which can fill the autumn air with their savour a hundred yards away.

A good way of catching the fruity tang of these wilding apples is to use them in an autumn pudding. Make this like a summer pudding, but substitute dark, autumnal fruits for the bright red raspberries and redcurrants.

Core, but don't peel, a pound of wilding apples and mix with about the same weight of blackberries, elderberries, stoned sloes, or whatever dark fruit is about. The precise ingredients and proportions aren't important; these seasonal fruit puddings should have the happenstance variety and spontaneity of a stockpot.

Cook for about a quarter of an hour, or until soft. Stir in dark honey to taste, and perhaps a pinch each of ground cumin and anise, as recommended by the French cook Gisèle Tronche in her wild fruit, 'humeur noir' jam recipes.

Transfer the pulp to a deep pudding basin lined with slices of brown wholemeal bread and use further slices until the pulp is absorbed and covered. Put a weight on top and leave in the refrigerator overnight, but remove half an hour before serving.

RICHARD MABEY is a writer and broadcaster specialising in rural and environmental topics. Author of 'Food for Free', Fontana/Collins, 1975.

APPLE, ORANGE AND LEMON DISH

This is a tasty dish made with Warner's King, Lord Derby or Bramleys. Remove strips of orange or lemon peel with a vegetable peeler, cut across into fine strips, place in cold water and bring to the boil. Cook until tender then rinse in cold water.

Take required number of apples, peel, core and finely slice apples. Butter a souffle dish, place about one inch of apples into the dish, sprinkle on some of the peel and a little demerara sugar, add more apple and peel until dish is full. Add a few knobs of butter, cover with greased paper and bake until apples are soft. Serve with whipped cream. Make plenty as apples shrink in cooking.

RUTH MOTT has cooked in many stately homes in England and appeared in the BBC series 'The Victorian Kitchen'.

BAKED FRUIT SALAD

This cooked fruit salad is based on one I ate in Lucca in Tuscany. It's really more of an idea than a recipe. Once you've got the knack, you can vary the types of fruit to your heart's content.

2 oranges
3 eating apples [Cox's Orange Pippin, Orleans Reinette or
Blenheim Orange]
3 pears [Williams, Doyenne du Comice or Passacrassana]
1 pineapple

2 bananas
8oz (225g) light muscovado sugar
2 ½fl oz (75ml) brandy or Grand Marnier
Serves 8

Line a large ovenproof dish with a double layer of silver foil. Divide the oranges, skin and all, into eighths. Core the apples and pears and cut into eighths. Peel the pineapple, and dice, discarding the woody core. Peel the bananas, and cut into chunks about 1½" (4cm) long. Mix all the fruit together well, and pack loosely into the dish.

Dredge with the sugar. Bake for 1 hour at 220C/425F/Gas 7, turning the fruit in its juices every 15 minutes or so. By the end of this time there should be edges here and there caught and blackened in the heat. Take out of the oven, and pour the brandy or Grand Marnier over. Leave to cool, basting occasionally with its own juices.

Serve with thick double cream, creme fraiche, or thick Greek yoghurt.

CREME NORMANDE

A marvellously rich and devastating pudding, that is simple to make. A small portion should be quite enough to satisfy each person after an ample meal, but if they are to follow a very light meal, you may find that there is only enough to go round four.

1lb (500g) scented eating apples, (Cox's Orange Pippin or Kidd's Orange Red)

4 tbsp Calvados or brandy
6 tbsp caster sugar
1 oz (30g) butter
3 egg yolks
10 fl oz (300ml) whipping cream
2 tbsp flaked almonds
Serves 6

Peel and core the apples. Chop roughly and toss in the Calvados. Set aside for 1 hour.

Drain off the Calvados and reserve. Either divide the apple pieces between 6 small ramekins or put them all into a single oven-proof dish. Dot with butter and sprinkle with half the sugar. Bake at 200C/400F/Gas Mark 6 for 20 minutes.

Mix the reserved Calvados with the remaining sugar, the egg yolks and the cream. Take the apples out of the oven, and pour this mixture over them. Scatter the flaked almonds over the top. Stand in a roasting tray, filled to a depth of 1" (25mm) with hot water, and return to the oven. Bake for a further 20-30 minutes, until the cream is almost set, but not quite solid. Serve hot, warm or cold.

SOPHIE GRIGSON from 'Sophie's Table', Michael Joseph, 1990. Author, food writer and cookery columnist for the London Evening Standard and the Sunday Express Magazine.

[You could try: King Offa Cider Brandy from Hereford Cider Museum, The Cider Mills, 21 Ryelands Street, Hereford. Somerset Royal Cider Brandy launched on Apple Day 1991, from Burrow Hill, Kingsbury Episcopi, Martock, Somerset.]

APPLE JACQUES PANCAKES

This is one of the most popular high tea-time recipes I know and is extremely easy. It's derived from a Normandy recipe and takes about as long to make as to read the instructions. The pancakes are fabulous served with lemon, honey or sugar, and are stupendous with apricot jam.

8oz (225g) apples - traditionally reinettes, but Ellison's
Orange is a good substitute
1 tbsp lemon juice
1 egg
1 tbsp oil
8oz (225g) plain flour
½pt (300ml) milk to mix
Serves 4

Grate the unpeeled apples and mix with the lemon juice. Beat the egg, oil and flour together and blend in the milk until the mixture is as smooth and thick as single cream. This usually takes about ½ pt (300ml) milk, but may vary according to the flour used. Stir in the apples. Drop the mixture in tablespoonfuls onto a hot greased griddle or frying pan. Each tablespoonful will form a thick 2½ inch (6cm) pancake. Turn the pancakes after 2 minutes and cook for another 90 seconds or so. Serve hot with apricot jam, honey, sugar or lemon.

MICHAEL BARRY, co-presenter on BBC's 'Food & Drink' series and author of 'Exotic Fast Food for the Crafty Cook', Ebury Press, 1991.

MISCELLANY

APPLE SORBETS

Tropical fruit sorbets are fashionable, but one can tire of their insistent flavours and vivid colours. For the very best sorbets, apples are hard to beat. In their infinite variety they provide a whole palette of colours, textures and aromas, as well as sorbets for every season. Even if you can't find the apples to serve a Cornish Aromatic sorbet, a D'Arcy Spice sorbet, a Melcombe Russet or a Green Balsam, consider the perfumed sweetness of a Worcester Pearmain sorbet, or the dry nuttiness of an Egremont Russet. A Granny Smith makes a marvellously tart, mouth-tingling sorbet and a really ripe flushed Golden Delicious a mouthful of sweetness.

To prepare apples for a sorbet, quarter and core them, then roughly chop, and put in a food processor or blender with a couple of tablespoons water and a teaspoon or two of lemon juice to stop discolouring. I like to keep a little of the peel on for the flecked effect it gives. Blend to a purée, and then mix with the syrup as described. I find it worthwhile keeping a bottle of syrup on hand for making sorbets. It is a sad fact that the smoothest textured sorbets have the most sugar.

Syrup:
2 1/2 lbs (1.10kg) sugar
1pt (580mls) water
Dissolve the sugar in the water over a low heat, then bring to the boil, and boil for 1 minute. Cool, then bottle and refrigerate.

Dilute the syrup with equal quantities of water, and add fruit pulp in equal volume to the liquid used. Stir in the juice of half a lemon. Blend thoroughly and freeze, either in an ice-cream maker or sorbetiere, according to the manufacturer's instructions. The mixture can also be frozen in a container put in the freezer or ice making part of the refrigerator. As the mixture freezes and crystals form, it will need to be stirred from time to time. To ensure a smooth sorbet, it is quite a good plan to give it its final stir in a food processor before putting it back in the freezer. Sorbets are best eaten within a few hours of being made.

I prefer to use raw apples, but interesting variations can be created with different apples cooked into a purée and then flavoured with cinnamon, cloves or cardamom. For another version, simply freeze cider into a sorbet or a coarser granita.

FRANCES BISSELL writes extensively about apples, as well as other ingredients, in the 'Sainsbury's Book of Food'. She is also The Times cook, with a column every Saturday.

NUTTY APPLE ICE

Kentish cobnuts are usually available from near the end of August until early October. I prefer those gathered from mid-September onwards, when the nuts are fully ripe, the shells and husks brown. These can be stored until Christmas in the fridge (or a very cold room) in a container to retain their moisture. Few people think of keeping them like this, but, after all, nuts are seeds which ripen in the autumn but germinate in spring, so mimicking a winter's soil should preserve them plump and crisp, ready to sprout once the cold weather is past. People used to store them in a tin buried in the garden.

This July I still had a few pounds left in a large covered bucket in a shed. Some were mouldy and a few had started to germinate, but the remainder were luscious, juicy and completely filling their shells, not at all like the yellowing withered kernels of imported filberts.

Nuts as a cooking ingredient should usually be roasted first. This greatly enhances their flavour so that only a few ounces, coarsely ground, lend a nutty tang to dishes savoury or sweet. Place them in an oven at 300F/150C/Gas 2 for up to an hour, depending on their size and freshness; but shell them first! As a child I sometimes threw nuts into bonfires, hoping they would explode, but usually only a disappointing muffled thud ensued. Putting them under a low grill is faster, but be vigilant, as they blacken only a moment after they have reached the desired stage of being hard and brittle.

Up to a fifth of the dry weight of cobnuts is protein, and there's the goodness in the apples, so you can pretend this lovely ice-cream is healthy eating!

1lb (480g) cooking apples [e.g. Warner's King, Beauty of Kent, George Neal]
1 tbsp water
Peel of half a lemon cut into strips
1 tbsp lemon juice
4 oz (120g)sugar
2 eggs (separated)
1/4pt (150ml) each single and double cream

1½ oz (40g) roasted coarsely-ground Kent cobnuts (you will probably need around 3½-4 oz (100g) of nuts in their shells to produce 1½ oz (40g) of roasted kernels, but be generous - they are so delicious that some may never reach the ice-cream!)

Cook the peeled apples with the water and lemon peel to a pulp in a tightly covered pan. Sieve, add lemon juice, sugar and beaten egg yolks and leave to cool. When cold mix in coarsely ground nuts, whip the egg whites until stiff and, using the same whisk, whip the single and double cream together. First fold the cream, then the egg whites, into the apple mixture and freeze in the fridge tray for 2 hours.

MEG GAME: writer, photographer and nut-grower.
Adapted from a recipe in 'Apple Recipes from A to Z' by Elizabeth Gili, Kaye Ward, 1975.

DORSET APPLE CAKE

This recipe for Dorset Apple Cake is one of my favourites. I would recommend the cooker Reverend W Wilks creamy-white, cooking to a pale yellow froth. It's a small tree, useful for gardens that can't accommodate a Bramley. It was introduced at the beginning of the century and named after the vicar of Shirley in Surrey, who invented the Shirley Poppy.

8oz (225g) flour
2oz (50g) butter
2oz (50g) lard/cooking fat

1lb (500kg) cooking apples (chopped)
4oz (100g) sugar
1 egg
2 tsp baking powder
a little milk

Mix all the ingredients well and bake in a cake tin in the oven for 45 minutes in a moderate oven around 350F/180C/Gas 4.

ANNA PAVORD: Broadcaster and Gardening Correspondent for The Independent and The Observer Magazine.

APPLE CAKE

8oz (225g) sugar
4oz (125g) butter (or soft margarine)
2 eggs - beaten
1/4tsp salt
8oz (225g) flour
1 level tsp baking powder
1 tbsp milk
1lb (500g) Cox's Orange Pippin apples - peeled and grated
2oz (50g) chopped nuts
1 teasp vanilla

Cream together sugar and butter.
Add beaten eggs.
Sift dry ingredients.
Add baking powder to the milk.

Add the dry ingredients and the milk alternately to the mixture.
Stir in grated apples and nuts.

Mix well. Add vanilla and mix.

Bake in a loaf tin in a moderate oven - 375F/190C/Gas 5 for 45 minutes.

HARRY BAKER is Fruit Officer at the Royal Horticultural Society Garden at Wisley. Author of 'The Fruit Garden Displayed', RHS, Cassell Ltd, 1986.

APPLE CAKE

1³/₄lb (800g) peeled, cored and quartered Cox's Orange Pippins
9oz (250g) unsalted butter
11oz (300g) caster sugar
7oz (200g) plain flour
6 whole eggs
1 sachet vanilla sugar
grated zest of one lemon
1 tsp ground cinnamon
1 tsp baking powder
Serves 6 or more

Stir fry the apples in 2 oz (50g) butter for 10 minutes. Add 4 oz (100g) caster sugar and a little of the zest of lemon and the cinnamon and continue to stir fry taking care not to break the apples. Set aside. In a bowl rub in 7 oz (200g) of soft butter to the flour. In a separate bowl beat the eggs with the sugar adding the baking powder and the rest of the zest. Now mix the two ingredients together and beat to obtain a very smooth paste. Butter a round baking dish 10" by 1" high and spread the mixture evenly in it. Put side by side the apple on top adding also the remaining juices. Put in a preheated oven and bake at medium heat for 25 minutes.

Allow the cake to cool and sprinkle with granulated sugar. It can also be eaten warm.

ANTONIO CARLUCCIO runs the Neal Street Restaurant in Covent Garden and is author of 'An Invitation to Italian cooking' and 'A Passion for Mushrooms' published by Pavilion. He is currently writing 'Antonio's Wild Food' to be published by Pavilion and 'Quick and Easy Pasta' for BBC Enterprises.

APPLE BREAD

A bread formed of "one third boiled apple pulp baked with two thirds flour having been properly fermented with yeast" was "excellent, full of eyes and extremely platable" wrote the eminent horticulturist John Claudius Loudon in his 'Encyclopedia of Gardening' in 1824.

The adding of apples to the dough makes a savoury bread which is good eaten with cheese. The following proportions are sufficient for one loaf.

12oz (350g) wholemeal flour

6oz (175g) apples, weighed after peeling and coring
½ oz (12g) fresh yeast (fresh yeast is easier than dried)
salt

Cook the apples to a purée. Blend the yeast to a smooth liquid with a little warm water - about half a teacupful. Add this to the warm, but not hot apple purée. Stir this into the salted flour and the resulting dough should be fairly moist. Leave it to rise and double its volume - about 1-2 hours. Then dust with flour, gather it together and work into a ball. Put this into the greased bread tin and leave to rise. When it reaches the top of the tin put it in an already hot oven. Bake 20 mins at 400F/210C/Gas 6 and 20 mins at 375F/190C/Gas 5. Turn out of the tin and let it cool.

JOAN MORGAN expert on apple varieties and author with Alison Richards of 'A Paradise out of a Common Field, the pleasures and plenty of the Victorian Garden', Century, 1990.

CRAB -APPLE JELLY

Just crab-apples and sugar

Wash the apples carefully and remove the stalks - no need to peel or core them. Put them into a pan, cover them with water and bring them to the boil.
Simmer away for about an hour or until the fruit goes pulpy. Strain the fruit through a muslin bag and leave to drip overnight. Measure the juice in the morning and for each pint of juice collected add 1lb (500g) of sugar.

Dissolve the sugar over a low heat, stirring carefully.
Bring to the boil and keep it there for the next 10 minutes before testing for setting.
Pour into warm jars, cover with a waxed piece of circular paper and then with cellophane kept in place with an elastic band.

ELIZABETH ASHFORD from 'What to do with an apple', Elizabeth Ashford, 1990.

DRYING APPLES

Not even the most fruit-avid children can deal with the quantity of apples given by a few productive trees in a good year. Perfect ones can be picked and stored for the winter, but some other method has to be employed for keeping blemished apples and windfalls. Poaching or puréeing, and freezing works well but takes up a lot of room in the freezer, and you have to cook.

Drying is an old method of preserving apples, and has the advantage of conserving and concentrating the flavour of the original variety. Dorothy Hartley's 'Food in England' describes how peeled and cored apples can be threaded on a string to make a long necklace which is dried out in a dry airy place. If a dry warm, well-aired store-room is available they can be kept like that, otherwise they must be sliced for storage.

Nowadays it is customary to core and slice the apples rings prior to drying on trays in a warm oven. A modern means is provided by a custom made drying machine called the Harvest Maid Dehydrator, which consists of circular trays which are loaded with fruit and stacked over a base which houses a small fan-heater. When the machine is switched on, the fan dryer, gently blows warm air through the trays. The standard five-tray version takes roughly a basketful of windfalls which will dry over-night on economy rate electricity.

The machine is worth its keep just for the smell. The resulting dried apples rings are very tasty and distinctive. They make a delicious sweetmeat (or they can be reconstituted, by adding water). Pears, and quince can also be dried; pear flavour is less good but the texture is interestingly gritty. Quince is grainier still, though not unpleasant and drying brings out the sweetness and tang of the fruit. It is possible to tell our Ribston Pippin rings from the Rosemary Russet and Lane's Prince Albert. The Lane's, quite sharp before drying, are possibly the best.

A particularly nice variation is to purée some apples and pour the purée in a thin layer on to a flexible plastic mat which fits on to each tray. It dries to a delicious leathery parchment which peels off when dry and can be rolled or stored flat. Cloves, nutmeg or cinnamon and different kinds of fresh chopped nuts can also be added.

(Harvest Maid Dehydrators are available at £108 (1991) including delivery from the International Supply Co., PO Box 189, Granary House, The Grange, St Peter Port, Guernsey, C.I.)

FRANCESCA GREENOAK, natural history and gardening writer and author of 'Forgotten Fruit', André Deutsch, 1983. She is Gardening Correspondent for The Times.

WASSAIL CUP

At one time in England and Wales most houses kept a wassail bowl ready throughout the Christmas festivities for unexpected guests. Carol singers carried their own cups to dip into the drink after they had sung.

Wassail comes from Old English 'wes hal', meaning 'be thou whole', and drinking from the wassail bowl was an expression of friendship; the custom of drinking your neighbour's good health probably came to be called toasting after the 'sippets' or pieces of toast floating in the wassail bowl.

Even the apple trees were wassailed to ensure a good crop. In Devon, on Twelfth Night, some farmers and their families still gather around the trees with shotguns or pots and pans. They make a tremendous noise to raise the Sleeping Tree Spirit and to scare off the demons. Then a toast is drunk and, for extra luck, some of the branches are dipped into the wassail bowl.

Pitmaston Pine Apple - a tiny juicy apple with a hint of pineapple - is my favourite of the thousands of British apples. With its yellow hued skin and miniature shape, it looks so appealing piled high on the Christmas table or, bobbing up and down in the Wassail Bowl.

8 small eating apples
32 cloves
2 1/2 pts (1.5 litres) brown ale
1/2 pt (300ml) sweet sherry
pinch of ground cinnamon

pinch of ground ginger
pinch of ground nutmeg
grated zest of 1 lemon
2 slices of bread, toasted
Serves 8

Slit the skin around the centre of the apples and stud them with cloves. Put them in a baking tin with ¼ pt (150ml) brown ale and bake in a 400F/200C/Gas 6 oven for about 30 minutes, basting occasionally.

Heat the remaining brown ale with the sherry, spices and lemon zest and simmer for about 5 minutes.

Cut the toast and the baked apples into small pieces, and serve the punch very hot, in a punch bowl, with the pieces floating on top.

HENRIETTA GREEN from 'Festive Food of England', Kyle Cathie, 1991. She is a food writer, broadcaster, publishes 'British Food Finds' and has a keen interest in the glories of British produce.

LOCAL APPLES AND CHEESES

We have lived in south-east Surrey for two years but so far no local cheesemaker's product has won our hearts. We cross the border into Sussex for three superlative cheeses; Castle Hill Farmhouse cheese is made near Rotherfield on the High Weald, a lovely nutty unpasteurised cheese that goes well with an old Sussex apple called Forge. Gospel Green cheese is another full flavoured partner for apples, and we like to associate the Egremont Russet with it, since Petworth House, which remains the seat of the Egremont family, is nearby. Near Pulborough is Malthouse Cottage Farm, where the Ferris family make several good goats' cheeses. Our favourite is Chancton, especially when this soft creamy cheese is really ripe - then the richly flavoured Cockle's Pippin is the apple to accompany it.

SIMONE SEKERS writes a cookery column in the Weekend Telegraph and Sunday Telegraph.

THE BLENHEIM ORANGE

In late November, I start looking around for a supplier of Blenheim Orange apples for Christmas. They are rarely available in the shops but there are still farms near us in Kent where one or two flourish in the corner of an orchard.

The Blenheim Orange is one of the largest dessert apples. It can sometimes be quite difficult to hold in one hand. It is usually round and regularly shaped, yellow coloured and streaked with red on the side that has faced the sun - a perfect picture book apple. The flesh is crisp and juicy, sweet, yet with a refreshing tang, rather like sweet cider.

This quality has made the Blenheim one of the few dual purpose apples. Its flesh will cook down rather like a new-season's

Bramley and, in 1831 it was described as a 'large noble sauce apple'.

Why do I like Blenheims at Christmas? Basically because Christmas and the days after tend to bring with them very large lunches. The only thing I can usually face in the evening is an apple and cheese. I like that apple to be special, and also substantial. I never cut apples up. I always munch them as though I have scrumped them out of an orchard, and eating two small apples means that you get too much core. One large one is a much better treat, especially if it is of a variety unavailable at other times of the year.

At Christmas it is a tradition in our house to buy a small truckle Cheddar cheese and large amounts of Stilton and Blue Cheshire. So, on Christmas night, after everyone has gone home or gone to bed, I curl up in an easy chair with a large Blenheim apple, a piece of each of my three cheeses and a glass of port. Bliss.

GAIL DUFF is a writer and broadcaster on cookery, country life and local customs.

SOURCES

APPLE DAY

Common Ground is working to encourage people to value and enjoy their own familiar surroundings, regardless of whether they are rare or unusual. We chose the apple as a symbol of the variety that we are losing in almost everything around us. If we lose the orchard we lose not only genetic variety, but also a way of life, the words that are associated with that place, the songs, the look and feel of the place and a lineage that goes back thousands of years. We impoverish our cultural landscape.

Our hope is that Apple Day will begin to be celebrated locally throughout the country on October 21, or the nearest weekend to it, to help make apparent the links between the apple and your landscape. Local ways of celebrating fruit may already exist, these may be worth reinventing if they are no longer practised. Some ideas follow - but you can start with an apple supper at home:

- Encourage local shops to stock local varieties for the day (and subsequently).
- Collect information for a local fruit recipe book or pamphlet - publish it and launch it with an orchard feast.
- Excite local pubs and restaurants to excel themselves with special menus and guest ciders.
- Encourage local horticultural societies and gardeners to give grafting and pruning demonstrations and run a swap shop.
- Add a new dimension to your autumn coffee morning: prepare a fruit feast and organise displays, tastings or competitions of local food and drink.
- Have a pippin party - taste varieties then plant the pips in pots

and gather each year until the trees fruit to see if you have a new rival for Cox's Orange...

- Organise an Apple Roadshow. Use local experts to help people to identify the varieties of apple in their garden and to diagnose the diseases which may be afflicting them.

- Celebrate wild fruits. Make a map of the wild crab apple, cherry, bullace, sloe and others, make sure they are cared for in hedgerow, garden and wood.

- Research and revive local traditions about orchards and apples

- Start collecting old songs and stories for a festival.

- There are customary games like apple bobbing, slicing, peeling and decorating - there may be local variations of these.

- Put on a play/performance/puppet show/poetry reading/music.

- Create new games - apple pie bed demonstrations and apple juggling.

- Organise an exhibition of photographs by local people of local orchards and portraits of fruit trees - domestic and wild.

- Organise orchard visits and walks.

- Run an Apple Hunt. Find out what apple varieties the locality has in its gardens and orchards, encourage their care.

- Organise wild life and mistletoe surveys in orchards.

SAVE OUR ORCHARDS

Why Conserve Old Orchards?

Orchards are important for many reasons:
- they create beautiful landscapes
- fruit trees are a source of good food - from apple pie to cider
- they can be valuable habitats for wild life - bees love fruit

blossom and blossom needs bees
- orchards and fruit trees are a rich source of poetic inspiration
- locally grown fruit provides local jobs and reduces transport costs - and pollution
- old varieties of fruit and wild fruit trees are irreplaceable sources of genetic diversity and may be or may parent the disease resistant strains of tomorrow
- orchards have a long tradition of multiple use - as places to graze sheep, geese and pigs, for the production of honey and as delightful places in which to stroll and rest
- they are imbued with local cultural significance. With communal effort, imagination and a little money, they can again become a valuable asset to the locality.

What To Do - New Life for Old Varieties

There are many ways in which we can begin to care for old orchards and fruit trees.

1) First of all find out what you have in your locality. Are there any orchards in your neighbourhood or parish? Are there many fruit trees growing in local gardens? Where are they and who is responsible for them?

2) Start a parish apple register or parish orchard map - noting the different varieties that grow in gardens, orchards and hedgerows. Record the area and number of trees. Search for varieties that are particular to your locality.

3) Trace the origins of varieties - especially those which have local associations. You might even discover a long lost variety.

Both the Brogdale Trust and Royal Horticultural Society have a fruit identification service (see later).

4) Campaign to save local orchards and fruit trees which are threatened by development. They are frequently undervalued by planners and farmers. Propose alternative uses - why not establish a community orchard?

5) Talk to the local farmer or grower. Find out if they have any old orchards that they are prepared to let or sell to the local community to care for and renovate. In Somerset, Devon and Gwent grants are available for the maintenance of traditional orchards - contact the Countryside Management team at your County or District Council about grants available in your area.

6) Encourage the retention, planting and care of wild and culti-vated fruit trees in hedgerows.

7) Find out if any local commercial orchards are open to the public. Some have annual open days (usually in September or October) when you are able to visit and taste the fruit.

8) Visit the nearest 'Pick Your Own' orchard and find out which varieties are grown. If they don't already have one, suggest they initiate a 'rent-a-tree' scheme involving local families and schools. Encourage them to grow local varieties and organise fruit tasting events.

9) Grow local varieties of fruit in your own garden. Consult our Gazetteer of Local Varieties as well as local growers and gardeners about varieties of fruit particular to your locality.

Take care to choose appropriate pollinators. Plant trees between November and March (before Christmas is preferable). Take grafts from your favourite old trees - it's not as difficult as it might seem at first.

10) Encourage shops to sell a wider range of local fruit and fruit products. Drink cider made from cider apples and perry from perry pears - obtain a copy of the 'Good Cider Guide' published by the Campaign for Real Ale. Rediscover and create recipes using local varieties of fruit. Make the most of the distinctive flavour and qualities of old varieties.

11) Set up a community orchard, re-establish a city orchard or create a school orchard. Encourage your local council to plant fruit trees on public land, in a corner of the park, on new estates, and on the edge of the town or city.

12) Celebrate Apple Day on October 21st.

GAZETTEER OF LOCAL VARIETIES

Take care when choosing fruit trees for your garden or orchard. By searching out varieties which have been widely grown in your locality in the past you are more likely to choose a tree which is better suited to local soils and climate. At the same time you will be helping to conserve cultural and genetic diversity and enhance the distinctive character of your place.

There are many varieties of fruit which have associations with particular places. Some have been discovered growing wild or have grown up as chance seedlings. Others have been introduced as a result of breeding by farmers, gardeners, nurserymen or scientists. In the seventeenth century John Gerarde found "every county and many parts of each county producing some sort or other of fruit not known in the next, or at least giving them other names." It is said that some varieties can only be grown to perfection in their place of origin. A variety might be peculiar to a particular parish, having only ever been grown in a very small area such as the perry pears of Gloucestershire and cherries of the Tamar Valley. Many varieties originally associated with a particular place have subsequently been planted over a wide area. Others have become extinct. Local associations are often revealed by their names - such as the Worcester Pearmain, Dittisham Plum and Galloway Pippin.

The following list is intended to help you make a start in selecting varieties of fruit you can grow to help conserve local diversity and enhance the distinctive character of your place. It is not comprehensive and being county-based, is just a general guide. Many of these varieties can be obtained from specialist nurseries. (Or why not graft your own from local trees?) Most are represented in the National Fruit Collections at Brogdale Orchards and can be grafted especially to order if unobtainable elsewhere. If you have any helpful comments or additions please let us know.

AVON: *apples* - Cheddar Cross, Beauty of Bath, Severn Bank
BEDFORDSHIRE: *apples* - Beauty of Bedford, Bedfordshire Foundling, Lord Lambourne, Laxtons Fortune, Laxton's Superb and others; *pear* - Wardon, Laxton's Early Market, Laxton's Foremost, Laxton's progress, Laxton's Record, Laxton's Superb;

plum - Fotheringham, Laxton's Gage and others

BERKSHIRE: *apples* - John Standish, Miller's Seedling, Charles Eyre, Charles Ross, Rival, Encore (culinary); *plum* - Marjorie's Seedling; *pear* - Williams' Bon Chrétien

BUCKINGHAMSHIRE: *apple* - Hambledon Deux Ans (raised in Hampshire); *damson* - Aylesbury Prune

CAMBRIDGESHIRE: *apple* - Allington Pippin (raised in Lincs), Chivers Delight, Histon Favourite, Barnack Beauty (raised in Northants), Emneth Early (culinary); *plum* - Cambridge Gage

CHESHIRE: *apple* - Arthur W. Barnes, Lord Derby (culinary); *damson* - Cheshire Prune

CLEVELAND:

CORNWALL: *apples* - Cornish Aromatic, Cornish Gilliflower, Glass Apple, Cornish Pine, Tommy Knight, Sops in Wine (cider), Plympton King (culinary); *plum* - Kea

CUMBRIA: *apple* - Carlisle Codlin, Keswick Codlin (found in Lancs), Forty Shilling, Beeley Pippin

DERBYSHIRE: *apple* - Newton Wonder (culinary)

DEVON: *apples* - Devonshire Quarrenden, Allspice, Michaelmas Stubbard, Crimson Costard, Star of Devon; *cider apples* - Brown's Apple, Sweet Coppin, Woodbine (Slack Ma Girdle), Tremlett's Bitter, Sweet Alford, Whitesour, Ponsford, Cerit, Ellis Bitter, Major; *plum* - Dittisham Ploughman; *cherries* - Dun, Large Black, Preserving, Small Black, Green Stemmed Black, Bottlers.

DORSET: *apple* - Melcombe Russet; *cider apple* - White Jersey; *plum* - Bryanston

DURHAM:

ESSEX: *apples* - D'Arcy Spice, George Cave, Waltham Abbey, Discovery, Queen, Chelmsford Wonder

GLOUCESTERSHIRE: *apples* - Ashmead's Kernel; *cider*

apples - Foxwhelp, Harvey, Bromsbury Crab, Must, Forest Styre; *plums* - Blaisdon Red, Dimmock Red

HAMPSHIRE: *apple* - Hambledon Deux Ans; *plum*- Angelina Burdett

HEREFORD: *apples* - King's Acre Pippin, Downton Pippin, Golden Harvey, Herefordshire Beefing, Lord Hindlip, Yellow Ingestrie; *cider apples* - Brown Snout, Foxwhelp, the Norman family; *perry pear* - Holme Lacey

HERTFORDSHIRE: *apples* - Lane's Prince Albert, Golden Reinette, Brownlees Russet, Bushey Grove, Hormead Pearmain (culinary); *cherries* - Caroon, Alba Heart, August Heart, Ronald's Heart, Smoky Heart, Strawberry Heart, Early Rivers

HUMBERSIDE: *pear* - Hessle

ISLE OF WIGHT: *apples* - Sir John Thorneycroft, Isle of Wight Pippin, Howgate Wonder (culinary)

ISLE OF MAN: *apple* - Manks Codlin

JERSEY: *cider apples* (some also used in the kitchen. Many originated in France) - Belles Filles, Capis, Douces Dames, Nier Binet, Petit Pigeonnet, Gros Pigeonnet, Romeril, Rouget (early and late), Tetard

KENT: *apples* - Kentish Fillbasket, Kent, Tydeman's Early, Late Orange, Greensleeves, Suntan, Mabbott's Pearmain, Beauty of Kent, Christmas Pearmain, Gascoyne's Scarlet, George Neal (culinary), Golden Knob, Maid of Kent, Bascombe's Mystery, Wanstall Pippin, and Warners King; *plums* - Bush, Black Diamond, Farleigh Damson; *cherries* - Frogmore Early, Nutberry Black, Kentish Red (culinary); *nuts* - Kent cob

LANCASHIRE: *apples* - Golden Spire, Roseberry (also known as Rosehill Pippin), Scotch Bridget, Proctor's Seedling; *culinary apples* - Sowman's Seedling, Pott's Seedling (raised in Cheshire)

LEICESTERSHIRE: *apples* - Annie Elizabeth, Queen Caroline

LINCOLNSHIRE: *apples* - Ellison's Orange, Herring's Pippin, Lord Burghley, Shakespeare, Peasgood's Nonsuch (culinary)

LONDON: *apples* - Cox's Orange Pippin, Fearn's Pippin, Langley Pippin, Hounslow Wonder, Rev. W. Wilks (culinary);

MANCHESTER: *apple* - Lord Suffield; *damson* - Cheshire Prune

MERSEYSIDE:

NORFOLK: *apples* - Hubbard's Pearmain, Baxter's Pearmain, Norfolk Beefing, Norfolk Royal, Norfolk Beauty, Robert Blatchford, Striped Beefing, Winter Coleman, Green Roland; *culinary apples* - Dr. Harvey, Golden Noble

NORTHAMPTONSHIRE; *apple* - Barnack Beauty

NORTHUMBERLAND:

NOTTINGHAMSHIRE: *apples* - Bess Pool, Bramley's Seedling (culinary)

OXFORDSHIRE: *apple* - Blenheim Orange

SHROPSHIRE: *apples* - Forester, Lady's Fingers

SOMERSET: *apple* - Hoary Morning (culinary); *cider apples* - Crimson King, Chisel Jersey, Cap of Liberty, Lambrook Pippin, Dabinett, Porter's Perfection, Stoke Red, White Jersey, Stembridge Jersey, Yarlinton Mill, Harry Masters Jersey, Tom Putt (cider and culinary); *pear* - Beurre d'Avalon

STAFFORDSHIRE:

SUFFOLK: *apples* - Sturmer Pippin, St. Edmund's Pippin, Lady Henniker; *plum* - Golden Drop

SURREY: *apples* - Claygate Pearmain, Cockle Pippin, George Carpenter, Joybells, Scarlet Nonpareil, King of the Pippins, Scarlet Crofton; *plum* - Crimson Drop

SUSSEX: *apples* - Alfriston (culinary), Crawley Beauty, Forge, Lady Sudeley, First and Last, Wadhurst Pippin

TYNE AND WEAR:

WARWICKSHIRE: *apples* - Wyken Pippin; *plum* - Warwickshire Drooper

WEST MIDLANDS: *apple* - Wyken Pippin

WILTSHIRE: *apples* - Roundway Magnum Bonum, Chorister Boy

WORCESTERSHIRE: *apples* - Pitmaston Pine Apple, May Queen, Betty Geeson, Worcester Pearmain; *plums* - Pershore (also known as Yellow Egg), Purple Pershore; *pear* - Black Worcester (culinary)

YORKSHIRE: *apples* - Green Balsam, Yorkshire Cockpit, Ribston Pippin, Flower of the Town, French Crab (Yorkshire Robin), Acklam Russett, Yorkshire Greening, Greenups Pippin (also known as Blob); *culinary pears* - Hessle, Wyedale; *plum* - Winesour

IRELAND (general): *apples* - Ard Cairn Russett, Ballorina Pippin, Bloody Butcher, Brown Crofton, Ecklinville Seedling, Irish Peach, Kerry Pippin, Ross Nonpareil, Sam Young, White Russett

IRELAND (north): *apples* - Ballyfatten, Barnhill Pippin, Dockney, Gibby's Apple, Greasy Pippin, Green Chisel, Keegan's Crab, Kemp, Martin's Seedling, Reid's Seedling, Sovereign, Strippy, Summer John, Thompson's Apple, Widow's Friend

IRELAND (south): *apples* - Clearheart, Dunkitt, Farrell, Honey Ball, Striped Brandy, Striped Sax, Tommy, Valentine

SCOTLAND: *apples* - Bloody Ploughman, Coul Blush (culinary), Early Julyan, Lady of the Wemyss, Stirling Castle, Tower of Glamis (culinary apple grown in the Carse of Gowrie, Clydesdale), White Melrose (from Melrose Abbey), James Grieve, Galloway Pippin (Wigtown, Galloway), Cambusnethan Pippin, Hawthornden (Edinburgh), Lass O'Gowrie, Oslin (also known

as the Arbroath Pippin); *pears* - Ayrshire Lass, Craig's Favourite, Green Pear of Yair
WALES: *apples* - Baker's Delicious (culinary), Saint Cecilia (from Monmouthshire); *cider apple* - Frederick.

With thanks to Harry Baker, James Armstrong Evans, George Morris, Trevor Pateman and Craig Pillans for their help in compiling this list.

SPECIALIST NURSERIES

This is a selective list of nurseries around the country which supply a wide range of fruit trees. As a first step it is best to go to the nursery nearest your home, but most nurseries will deliver trees to your door. Some nurseries are prepared to graft to order, with varieties and rootstocks of your choice (see those marked*).

ABERDEENSHIRE - Springhill Nurseries Ltd, Lang Stracht, Aberdeen (0224 693788)
BERKSHIRE - J.C. Allgrove, The Nursery, Middle Green, Lampley, Slough, (0753 20155)
CAMBRIDGESHIRE - P J Nurseries, 26 Church View, High Street, Oakington (0223 234757)
CHESHIRE - Bridgemere Nurseries Ltd, Bridgemere, Nr Nantwich (09365 239)
CHESHIRE - Morrey and Son, Forest Nursery, Kelsall, nr Tarporley (0829 51342)
DEVON - W H Harris, Westacott Nursery, Barnstaple (0271 3762)

DEVON - St Bridget Nurseries, Old Rydon Lane, Exeter (039287 3672)

DEVON - Everard O'Donnell, Redhill Farm, Burlescombe, Tiverton - culinary, dessert and cider apples (0823 672244)*

ESSEX - W Seabrook and Sons Ltd, Little Leighs Hall, Little Leighs, Chelmsford (024534 221/462)

GLOUCESTERSHIRE - Highfield Nurseries, Whitminster, Gloucester (0452 740266)

HAMPSHIRE - Blackmoor Fruit Nurseries, Blackmoor, Liss (04203 3576)

HAMPSHIRE - Deacon's Nursery, Godshill, Isle of Wight, (0983 840750)

HAMPSHIRE - Family Trees, PO Box 3, Botley (0489 895674)

HEREFORDSHIRE - Bulmers, The Cider Mills, Plough Lane - cider apples (0432 352000)

HERTFORDSHIRE - Aylett's Nurseries Ltd, North Orbital Rd, St Albans (0727 22255)

KENT - Keepers Nursery, 446 Wateringbury Road, East Malling, Maidstone (0622 813008)*

KENT - New Tree Nurseries, 2 Nunnery Road, Canterbury (0227 761209)*

LINCOLNSHIRE - Eden Nurseries, Rectory Lane, Old Bolingbroke, Spilsby (07903 582)

NORFOLK - Chris Bowers & Sons, Whispering Trees Nursery, Wimbotsham (0366 388752)

SOMERSET - Scotts Nurseries Ltd, Merriott (0460 72306)*

WORCESTERSHIRE - F.P. Matthews Ltd, Berrington Court, Tenbury Wells (0584 810214)

YORKSHIRE - R.V. Roger Ltd, The Nurseries, Pickering (0751 72226)

SPECIALIST SUPPLIERS OF FRUIT

This is a selection of the many farm shops and Pick Your Own farms around the country which grow and supply a wide range of tree fruit. A further list can be found in 'Orchards - a guide to local conservation', Common Ground or write, enclosing a s.a.e. to the Farm Shop and Pick Your Own Association, Agriculture House, Knightsbridge, London, SW1X 7NJ for a booklet listing many more places.

If you cannot get the apples you require from your local greengrocer suggest that they get the wallchart from the British Independent Fruit Growers Association (BIFGA) showing wholesale distributors of some of the more unusual varieties of apple: BIFGA, Staplehurst, Tonbridge, Kent TN12 0EX.

CHESHIRE- Haworth's Fruit Farm, Yeld Lane, Kelsall, (0829 51188) - 16 varieties, farm shop and Pick Your Own.
DEVON - Kim Wilson-Gough, Whitestone Farm, East Cornworthy, Totnes, (080 422400) - organic, selection of old and Devon varieties available in season, farm shop and mail order. (Natural Fruit Growers Association, wholesale only).
ESSEX - Crapes Fruit Farm, Aldham, Colchester, (0206 212375) - grow over 150 varieties, including Ribston Pippin, Orleans Reinette, Red Ellison, farm shop and by mail order.
ESSEX - Olivers Orchard, Olivers Lane, Colchester, (0206 330208) - several varieties including D'Arcy Spice, cherry, pear, quince, plum, Pick Your Own and farm shop.
HAMPSHIRE - Blackmoor Estate Ltd, Blackmoor, Liss (0420 473782) - several varieties, ring farm shop for availability.
HEREFORDSHIRE - Breinton Manor Fruit Farm, Hereford

(0432 265271) - over 20 varieties of apple and pear, farm shop from September to April.

HEREFORDSHIRE - Priors Grove, Putley, Ledbury (053 183511) - 10 varieties plus pears, farm shop also supplies shops and supermarkets (organic).

HERTFORDSHIRE- Littlefield Farm, Kinsbourne Green Lane, Harpenden (0582 765027) - 5 varieties, James Grieve, Chivers Delight, also Rent-a-Tree scheme.

KENT - Brogdale Farm, Brogdale Road, Faversham (0795 535286) thousands of varieties in season, plus cherry, pear, plum, soft fruit, etc., farm shop.

KENT - Hewitts Farm, Chelsfield, Orpington (0959 34271) - 41 varieties including Ashmead's Kernel, King of the Pippins and Orleans Reinette, farm shop and pick your own.

KENT - Perry Court, Bilting, Ashford (0233 812408) - 30 varieties of apple and pear, farm shop.

NORFOLK - Websters of Roughton, Thorpe Market Road, Roughton (0263 833777) - new orchard growing 22 varieties.

OXFORDSHIRE - Grove Farms, Milton Hill, Abingdon (0235 820753/831575) - 20 varieties including Blenheim Orange and Queen Cox, farm shop.

SOMERSET- Charlton Orchards, Creech St Michael, Taunton (0823 412979) - 17   varieties also pear, plum and damson.

SUFFOLK - Sweetapples Orchard, Stowupland, Stowmarket (0449 674791) - several varieties, farm shop (organic).

SURREY - Royal Horticultural Society Gardens, Wisley, Ripley (0483 224234) - Surplus fruit from the gardens sold in season at the Fruit Shop.

SUSSEX - Hunts Fruit, Sharewood Farm, New England Lane, Seddlescombe, Battle (0424 870354) - 150 varieties grown including, Kidd's Orange Red, Spartan and Crispin, farm shop

WARWICKSHIRE - Snitterfield Fruit Farm, Kings Lane, Stratford-upon-Avon (0789 731244) - 19 varieties, farm shop.
WORCESTERSHIRE - Walsgrove Fruit Farm, Egdon, Spetchley (090565 371) - 60 varieties including Cockle Pippin, Peasgood's Nonsuch and Beauty of Bath.
YORKSHIRE - Ampleforth College Orchards, Ampleforth College, Ampleforth (04393 485) - 57 varieties grown, chemical free, farm shop September - March.

APPLE IDENTIFICATION

The gnarled apple (or other fruit) tree you have in your garden may be the last of a unique variety - one which has adapted to your particular soil and climate conditions. Please find out what variety your tree is before you consider grubbing it up, it may not be a September eater, but a May cooker if stored well, and it may be perfectly happy growing horizontally. Others may like to take grafts from your tree. Ask previous owners, neighbours and local enthusiasts what they know about your trees.

To have your apples identified, send 1-3 typical, mature fruits with stalk from the same tree plus leaves and twigs carefully packed in paper in a strong box (not a soap box - smell is important in identification) to one of the addresses below.

Remember to number the varieties and your trees so you know which is which when the reply comes and to include your name, address and telephone number in block capitals. Add any useful information like the age of the tree if known, how tall it is, where it is growing, in what soil, how often it bears fruit, when picked.

Miss Mary Ellis, The Brogdale Horticultural Trust, Brogdale Road, Faversham, Kent ME13 8XZ (send £5.88 per apple, for five samples, then each additional sample £2.94.)

The Royal Horticultural Society, Fruit Identification Department, Wisley, Ripley, Surrey GU23 6QB (send £2 for first apple, £1 for each subsequent apple, plus s.a.e. for reply).

Both Brogdale and the RHS grow hundreds of dessert and culinary apples in their collections and are well worth joining and visiting.

If you know the apple tree has been raised from a pip it will be an entirely new variety - do not send it - name it yourself.

FURTHER READING

John Bultitude, 'Apples', MacMillan Press, 1988.
Lawrence D Hills, 'The Good Fruit Guide', Henry Doubleday Research Association, 1984.
David Kitton (Ed.), 'The Good Cider Guide', Alma Books (CAMRA), 1990.
Rosanne Sanders, 'The English Apple', Phaidon Books, 1989.
Common Ground, 'Orchards - a guide to local conservation', Common Ground, 1989.
Muriel Smith, 'The National Apple Register', MAFF, 1971.
Jane Grigson, 'Jane Grigson's Fruit Book', Penguin, 1982.
F.A. Roach, 'Cultivated Fruits of Britain - their origin and history', Blackwell, 1985.

ABOUT COMMON GROUND

Common Ground is working to encourage new ways of looking at the world, to excite people into remembering the richness of the commonplace and the value of the everyday, to savour the symbolisms with which we have endowed nature, to revalue our emotional engagement with places and all that they mean to us and to go on to become actively involved in their care.

We have chosen to focus attention not singularly upon natural history or archaeology or social history or legend or literary traditions but upon their complex combining which is the reality of people's relationship with their places, and which begins in our hearts but gets mediated by our reason.

In attempting to reassert the importance of liberating our subjective response to the world about us we have turned for philosophical help to those who wear their emotions on their sleeve. We work with people from all branches of the arts. Much of what we do attempts to place cultural arguments and evidence beside the scientific, technical and economic rationales which so dominate, and often debilitate our ways of thinking and doing.

Common Ground is a charity which does not have a membership. Our hope is that using our projects and ideas will help people to become more involved for themselves in their own localities. We are funded by a wide variety of charitable trusts, government agencies, businesses and individuals. Our charity number is: 326335.

COMMON GROUND PUBLICATIONS

Apple Day, Save our Orchards, Community Orchards, Tree Dressing Day, Parish Maps pamphlets each 50p + s.a.e.

Apple Map, with illustrations by Kate Charlesworth and Charles Raymond and descriptions of many varieties of apples county by county, (colour A1 poster), £6.00 + £1 p&p.

Apple Day postcard, one of a set of six festival cards, £4.50 for a set of six mixed or single design.

Apple Games & Customs, text by Beatrice Mayfield, foreword by Sophie Grigson, illustrations by Geraldine Bracey, Common Ground, 1994, £5.95 + £1 p+p.

Orchards: a guide to local conservation, Common Ground, 1989, £4.95 + 1.05 p+p.

The Apple Broadcast, 16 page, A3 newspaper, Common Ground, 1994, £2.00 incl. p+p.

In a Nutshell: a manifesto for trees and a guide to growing and protecting them, Neil Sinden with drawings by David Nash, Common Ground, 1989, £6.95 + £1.40 p+p.

Trees Be Company: a poetry anthology edited by Angela King and Sue Clifford for Common Ground, Bristol Press, 1990, £5.95 + 1.40 p+p.

Celebrating Local Distinctiveness, Common Ground for Rural Action, 1994, £2.20 incl. p+p.

Common Ground Rules for Local Distinctiveness - an ABC of the locally particular from Ayrshire Cows to Zennor Church, (illustrated broadsheet, A2) £4.50 incl. p+p.

Available from:

Common Ground
41 Shelton Street
London WC2H 9HJ